# Credit
# Language
## A SURVIVAL VOCABULARY

**Jim Richey**
**Reading Specialist**

**Illustrated by Donna Nettis**

GLOBE FEARON

Pearson Learning Group

**Janus Survival Vocabulary Books**
Banking Language
Clothing Language
Credit Language
Driver's License Language
Drugstore Language
Entertainment Language
Job Application Language
Medical Language
Restaurant Language
Supermarket Language

ISBN 0-8359-1522-0
Printed in the United States of America

5 6 7 8    09 08 07 06

Globe Fearon
Pearson Learning Group

1-800-321-3106
www.pearsonlearning.com

# Contents

# Introduction

Imagine this . . .

You just had a phone call. That job you wanted is yours. All you have to do is be there Monday. This is your big chance to make some real money.

Then it hits you. *What to wear?* This job calls for some pretty fancy clothes. A quick look in your closet shows you nothing. That means you'll have to buy some new clothes. But you don't have much money!

You find a store that has what you want. They may let you take the clothes now and pay later. That's called *buying on credit* (KRED uht)*.

But first there are some long forms you'll have to fill in and sign. Full of words you don't know. Better not sign the forms until you know what those words mean.

That's where this book comes in. It will show you what those words mean. Then you'll know if you should sign those forms or not.

Who knows? Maybe you'll really get that phone call we talked about. So turn the page and get yourself ready. Your phone could ring tonight. . . .

---

*You will see a respelling like this after many words in this book. To learn how to use the respellings, see page 48.

**Down payment**   The man above would like to buy the big boat and pay for it later. But first, he must pay a down payment, or a part of the cost.

How much is the down payment for the boat?

_____

## Pretest

- [ ] date
- [ ] loan
- [ ] rate
- [ ] cost
- [ ] due
- [ ] terms
- [ ] firm
- [ ] risk
- [ ] type
- [ ] owed
- [ ] charge
- [ ] source
- [ ] spouse
- [ ] debt
- [ ] gross

**Can I get a loan to buy a horse?**

## Words and Meanings

Say the credit word out loud and read its meaning. Read the sentence that follows. Then find and circle the credit word in the sentence. The first one is done for you.

**Date** (DAYT): *day, month, and year.*

The (date) this country started was July 4, 1776.

**Loan** (LOHN): *money lent to you.*

Can I get a loan to buy a horse?

**Rate** (RAYT): *how much you pay for each dollar of the loan.*

My bank's rate for loans is 12 cents for each dollar.

**Cost** (KAWST): *price of something.*

What was the cost of your new bike?

**Due** (DOO): *date when something has to be paid.*

Today is the day your loan is due.

## Same Words

Check the word in each row that is the same as the first word in the row. Go as fast as you can. Time yourself. The first one is done for you.

| | | | | |
|---|---|---|---|---|
| **Due** | Hue | Blue | Due ✓ | Cue |
| **Rate** | Date | Rate | Bait | Late |
| **Loan** | Loan | Lone | Moan | Load |
| **Date** | Rate | Date | Fate | Gate |
| **Cost** | Most | Coast | Close | Cost |

No. Correct _____

Time _____

# Scrambled Letters

The letters in each of the words are mixed up. Write the letters so they form words from the list at the top of page 7. The first one is done for you.

soct _____ *cost* _____

tead _____

nola _____

ued _____

tare _____

# Missing Vowels

To finish the word, fill in the missing vowels. Write the complete word on the blank lines. The first one is done for you.

de _____ *due* _____

ln _____

dt _____

cst _____

rt _____

# Pick a Word

Underline the word that belongs in the space. Then write the word in the space. The first one is done for you.

July 4, 1776, is a _____ *date* _____ .
    debt        <u>date</u>        rate

Go to the bank for a _____ .
    cone        lone        loan

Pay the bill when it is _____ .
    due        done        doe

How much does that _____ ?
    coast        gross        cost

The cost of a loan is its _____ .
    safe        limit        rate

**That firm makes what you need.**

# Words and Meanings

Say the credit word out loud and read its meaning. Read the sentence that follows. Then find and circle the credit word in the sentence.

**Terms** (TERMZ): *rules you must follow.*

Go along with the bank's terms, or it won't give you a loan.

**Firm** (FERM): *a company.*

That firm makes what you need.

**Risk** (RISK): *the chance of a loss.*

The bank takes a risk when it lends money.

**Type** (TIGHP): *a kind or sort.*

That type of loan costs more than this one.

**Owed** (OHD): *had to pay.*

I paid the bank the money I owed it.

# Same Words

Check the word in each row that is the same as the first word in the row. Go as fast as you can. Time yourself.

| | | | | |
|---|---|---|---|---|
| **Risk** | Rink | Rise | Frisk | Risk |
| **Terms** | Terms | Times | Germs | Teams |
| **Owed** | Owned | Owed | Old | Owl |
| **Type** | Pipe | Hype | Tire | Type |
| **Firm** | Fire | Firm | Term | Harm |

No. Correct _____

Time _____

## Word Wheel

Begin at Start. Find the word. Put a line between it and the next word. One word follows another. Write the words on the lines as you find them. The first one is done for you.

_TYPE_

_____

_____

_____

_____

Start ▶ T Y P E / T E R M S O W E D R I S K F I R M

## Missing Ink

Complete the words below by adding a curve or a straight line to each letter. Then write the words on the lines. The first one is done for you.

R I S K _____ _RISK_____

Г ı R M _____

O V I Ɔ _____

T E R M S _____

Г Y P E _____

## Pick a Word

Underline the word that belongs in the space. Then write the word in the space.

There is more than one _____ of loan.
    type        date        time

He _____ money to the bank.
    sold        billed        owed

A _____ is a place of work.
    date        firm        credit

Banks want you to follow their _____ .
    time        safe        terms

Don't take a _____ . Lock your door.
    risk        debt        total

**Will this be cash or charge?**

## Words and Meanings

Say the credit word out loud and read its meaning. Read the sentence that follows. Then find and circle the credit word in the sentence.

**Charge** (CHAHRJ): *take now and pay later.*

Will this be cash or charge?

**Source** (SORS): *where something comes from.*

The bank was the source of this loan.

**Spouse** (SPOWS): *person you're married to.*

Have you and your spouse been married long?

**Debt** (DET): *money you owe.*

After paying your debt, you won't owe any money.

**Gross** (GROHS): *all the money you make.*

Your gross pay isn't enough to buy that car.

## Same Words

Check the word in each row that is the same as the first word in the row. Go as fast as you can. Time yourself.

| | | | | |
|---|---|---|---|---|
| **Spouse** | Source | Spouse | Souse | Spout |
| **Debt** | Date | Due | Debt | Debit |
| **Source** | Source | Spouse | Sauce | Sort |
| **Gross** | Grass | Goes | Grows | Gross |
| **Charge** | Change | Chart | Charge | Clang |

No. Correct _____

Time _____

## Letter Circles

The letters in each circle at right spell a word from the list at the top of page 11. Write the word below the circle. One is done for you.

## Missing Vowels

To finish the word, fill in the missing vowels. Write the complete word on the blank lines.

grss _____

src _____

dbt _____

sps _____

chrg _____

## Pick a Word

Underline the word that belongs in the space. Then write the word in the space.

When you owe money, you are in _____ .
    date             debt          agreement

You pay later when you _____ something.
    charge         loan         limit

Where a thing comes from is its _____ .
    terms         total        source

A wife or a husband is a _____ .
    sport        finance      spouse

_____ pay is what you get before taxes.
    Gross        Unit        Item

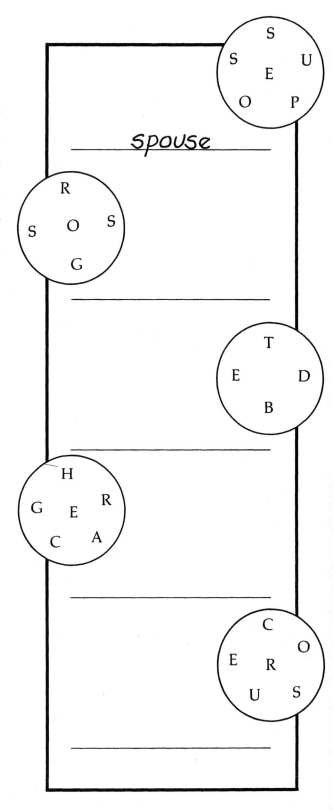

_spouse_

# Review

The 15 words listed below are hidden in the puzzle. They are all printed in a straight line. But the line may read across, up, down, backwards, or on a slant. Some of the words overlap.

Circle the words as you find them. Then cross them off your list. One word is done for you.

| | |
|---|---|
| ~~DATE~~ | TYPE |
| RATE | OWED |
| COST | CHARGE |
| DUE | SOURCE |
| LOAN | SPOUSE |
| TERMS | DEBT |
| FIRM | GROSS |
| RISK | |

```
N T I W O S L O A N T T M I D
D O M O O S G R A O E L F E U
M T A O C P O E M R T T O H E
R A I T D O O F M S T R H I E
I P R A E U Y S T T O H Q E U
F I K B C S W R O N Z U O X J
Y E O D V E M T P E H L R Z A
Y D P O R E G S N I E D T C J
R I S K L T O R T Y P E N D E
I W M A M E W Y M C O A A R L
T E E I R S E T H G R O S S E
D E B T D I D E T N O F H E T
V I S C E S P N A O T S T E U
E O T D D R X I S P A E T A R
C H A R G E E R U B I O A D M
```

---

# Test

Put a + by the sentence that is true. Put a ○ by the sentence that is not true. One is done for you.

___+___ 1. A bank may be the source of a loan.

_____ 2. The cost of a loan is its rate.

_____ 3. There is more than one type of loan.

_____ 4. A wife or a husband is a gross.

_____ 5. You pay now when you charge something.

_____ 6. The due date is when you have to pay a loan.

_____ 7. A firm is the same as a risk.

_____ 8. If you owed money, you were in debt.

_____ 9. A spouse is a type of loan.

_____ 10. Most loans have terms you must follow.

# Unit Two

**Charge plans**    Some stores have charge plans. People in the plan buy things without paying cash. They pay later when they get a bill. When will the woman above pay?

_____

## Pretest

- [ ] borrow
- [ ] total
- [ ] equal
- [ ] item
- [ ] limit
- [ ] lender
- [ ] savings
- [ ] billing
- [ ] unpaid
- [ ] income
- [ ] assets
- [ ] contract
- [ ] current
- [ ] statement
- [ ] monthly

**What is the cost of that item?**

# Words and Meanings

Say the credit word out loud and read its meaning. Read the sentence that follows. Then find and circle the credit word in the sentence.

**Borrow** (BAHR oh): *to take or use something you agree to give back later.*

You can borrow money now and pay it back later.

**Total** (TOH tuhl): *everything added up.*

The total cost of all three gifts is $10.

**Equal** (EE kwuhl): *the same as.*

$100 a month is equal to $1200 a year.

**Item** (IGH tuhm): *one separate thing.*

What is the cost of that item?

**Limit** (LIM uht): *as far as you can go; the end.*

The limit on your charge plan is $500.

# Same Words

Check the word in each row that is the same as the first word in the row. Go as fast as you can. Time yourself.

| | | | |
|---|---|---|---|
| **Borrow** | Burrow | Bower | Borrow |
| **Equal** | Equal | Equate | Annual |
| **Limit** | Item | Lime | Limit |
| **Total** | Tote | Total | Title |
| **Item** | Term | Time | Item |

No. Correct _____

Time _____

# Word Wheel

Begin at Start. Find the word. Put a line between it and the next word. One word follows another. Write the words on the lines as you find them.

_____

_____

_____

_____

_____

Start ▶ I T E M B O R R O W E Q U A L L I M I T T O T A L

# Scrambled Letters

The letters in each of the words are mixed up. Write the letters so they form words from the list at the top of page 15.

mite _____

loatt _____

leauq _____

robwor _____

tilim _____

# Pick a Word

Underline the word that belongs in the space. Then write the word in the space.

You can't spend more than your _____ .
     limit        charge        type

To get the _____ cost, add the price of each thing.
     total        terms        loan

You _____ things you agree to give back.
     item        steal        borrow

Things that are _____ are the same.
     due        equal        gross

An _____ is just one thing.
     loan        item        debt

**All unpaid bills must be paid soon.**

# Words and Meanings

Say the credit word out loud and read its meaning. Read the sentence that follows. Then find and circle the credit word in the sentence.

**Lender** (LEN der): *a person or bank you borrow from.*

When the bank gives a loan, it is the lender.

**Savings** (SAYV ingz): *money saved.*

I keep my savings at the People's Bank.

**Billing** (BILL ing): *sending a bill.*

The billing date shows this bill was sent two months ago.

**Unpaid** (uhn PAYD): *not paid.*

All unpaid bills must be paid soon.

**Income** (IN kuhm): *all the money you make.*

My income is not enough to pay for this car.

# Same Words

Check the word in each row that is the same as the first word in the row. Go as fast as you can. Time yourself.

| | | | |
|---|---|---|---|
| **Income** | Interest | Income | Item |
| **Savings** | Safety | Saves | Savings |
| **Billing** | Building | Billing | Bills |
| **Lender** | Lender | Leader | Loader |
| **Unpaid** | Unit | Umpire | Unpaid |

No. Correct _____

Time _____

## Missing Ink

Complete the words below by adding a curve or a straight line to each letter. Then write the words on the lines.

UNPAID _____

LENDER _____

INCOME _____

SAVINGS _____

BILLING _____

## Missing Vowels

To finish the word, fill in the missing vowels. Write the complete word on the blank lines.

svngs _____

ncm _____

bllng _____

npd _____

lndr _____

## Pick a Word

Underline the word that belongs in the space. Then write the word in the space.

You can keep your _____ in a bank.

    spouse       savings       charge

The _____ date shows when a bill was sent.

    billing       total       risk

You borrow money from a _____ .

    debt       gross       lender

The money you make is your _____ .

    purchase       income       account

Please pay all your _____ bills.

    equal       unpaid       savings

**The bank mails me a statement every month.**

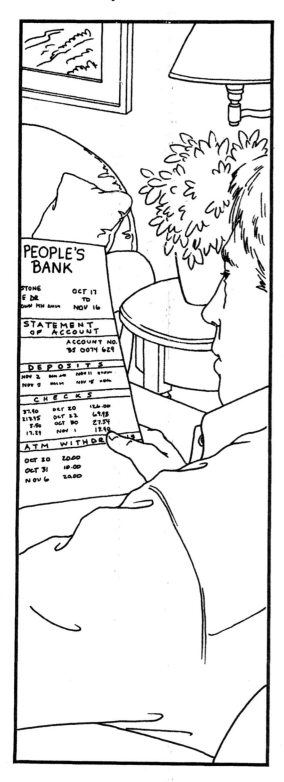

## Words and Meanings

Say the credit word out loud and read its meaning. Read the sentence that follows. Then find and circle the credit word in the sentence.

**Assets** (AS ets): *everything you own.*

Assets are things like money, cars, and houses.

**Contract** (KON trakt): *a paper telling what you agree to.*

Remember! Your contract says you will pay on the 15th of the month.

**Current** (KER uhnt): *up to date; now.*

Your current pay is how much you make now.

**Statement** (STAYT muhnt): *a notice that shows what you paid and what you owe.*

The bank mails me a statement every month.

**Monthly** (MUHNTH lee): *once a month.*

The store will bill you monthly.

## Same Words

Check the word in each row that is the same as the first word in the row. Go as fast as you can. Time yourself.

| | | | |
|---|---|---|---|
| **Current** | Current | Comment | Contract |
| **Statement** | Statue | Statement | Cement |
| **Assets** | Assures | Aspects | Assets |
| **Monthly** | Money | Monkey | Monthly |
| **Contract** | Current | Contract | Contact |

No. Correct _____

Time _____

## Missing Ink

Complete the words below by adding a curve or a straight line to each letter. Then write the words on the lines.

CURRENT _____

MONTHLY _____

ASSETS _____

CONTRACT _____

STATEMENT _____

## Missing Vowels

To finish the word, fill in the missing vowels. Write the complete word on the blank lines.

sttmnt _____

ssts _____

crrnt _____

mnthly _____

cntrct _____

## Pick a Word

Underline the word that belongs in the space. Then write the word in the space.

_____ bills are due at the end of each month.

Monthly           Equally           Rate

Your _____ are everything you own.

debts           savings           assets

_____ means up to date.

Late           Current           Loan

A _____ shows what you've paid and what you owe.

rate           statement           spouse

A _____ shows what you agree to do.

contract           firm           source

# Review

The 15 words from the list on page 14 fit into this puzzle. They go across and down. The sentences and number of spaces will help you. As you find the words, write them in the spaces in the sentences. One is done for you.

## Across

3. _Monthly_ bills are paid once a month.

6. An _____ is one thing.

8. A _____ shows if you owe anything.

9. _____ means up to date.

11. _____ are kept in a bank.

13. Money you make is your _____.

14. You add to get a _____.

## Down

1. A _____ shows what you agree to do.

2. _____ bills haven't been paid.

4. You borrow from a _____.

5. Your _____ are what you own.

7. Things that are _____ are the same.

10. The _____ date shows when a bill was sent.

12. You _____ something you agree to give back later.

15. You can't spend more than your _____.

(Crossword grid: 3 Across = MONTHLY)

# Test

Put a + by any sentence that is true. Put a ○ by any sentence that is not true.

_____ 1. Your monthly income is the money you get each month.

_____ 2. Money you borrow has to be paid back.

_____ 3. A statement shows how much you owe.

_____ 4. *Current* means "unpaid."

_____ 5. An item is the same as a billing.

_____ 6. Money that you spend is called savings.

_____ 7. A contract says what you agree to do.

_____ 8. Your total assets equal everything you owe.

_____ 9. A bank can be a lender.

_____ 10. It is OK to spend over a limit.

# Unit Three

**Credit cards** Some companies and banks lend money through credit cards. People use the credit card, instead of money, to buy things. Then they pay what they owe to the company or bank. How many different cards does the place above take?

_____

## Pretest
- [ ] advance
- [ ] business
- [ ] amount
- [ ] account
- [ ] balance
- [ ] finance
- [ ] purchase
- [ ] increase
- [ ] earnings
- [ ] interest
- [ ] confirmed
- [ ] cancelled
- [ ] bankrupt
- [ ] default
- [ ] reference

**He works for a business that paints cars.**

## Words and Meanings

Say the credit word out loud and read its meaning. Read the sentence that follows. Then find and circle the credit word in the sentence.

**Advance** (ad VANS): *ahead of time.*

Please pay this bill in advance.

**Business** (BIZ nuhs): *a firm; a company.*

He works for a business that paints cars.

**Amount** (uh MOWNT): *how much.*

This bill shows me the amount of money I owe.

**Account** (uh KOWNT): *a kind of plan.*

I have a charge account at this store, and a savings account at the bank.

**Balance** (BAL uhns): *how much you still owe.*

After paying $10, I still owe a balance of $25.

## Same Words

Check the word in each row that is the same as the first word in the row. Go as fast as you can. Time yourself.

| | | | |
|---|---|---|---|
| **Advance** | Admit | Assets | Advance |
| **Account** | Amount | Count | Account |
| **Balance** | Balance | Business | Ballast |
| **Amount** | Account | Amount | Annual |
| **Business** | Busy | Balance | Business |

No. Correct _____

Time _____

# Word Wheel

Begin at Start. Find the word. Put a line between it and the next word. One word follows another. Write the words on the lines as you find them.

_____

_____

_____

_____

_____

Start ▶ A M O U N T A D V A N C E B U S I N E S S A C C O U N T B A L A N C E

# Missing Ink

Complete the words below by adding a curve or a straight line to each letter. Then write the words on the lines.

bJSʼNESS _____

AMOJNT _____

BALANCE _____

ACCOUNT _____

ADVANCE _____

# Pick a Word

Underline the word that belongs in the space. Then write the word in the space.

A firm is a _____ .
    source        assets        business

The _____ of a loan is what you owe.
    balance        lender        unit

Do you have a charge _____ at this store?
    statement        account        charge

A bill shows the _____ of money you owe.
    unit        current        amount

To pay a bill in _____ is to pay before it is due.
    advance        item        interest

**We'd like to make a purchase, please.**

# Words and Meanings

Say the credit word out loud and read its meaning. Read the sentence that follows. Then find and circle the credit word in the sentence.

**Finance** (FIGH nans): *having to do with money or credit.*

Sometimes you pay a finance charge when you use credit.

**Purchase** (PER chuhs): *anything you buy.*

We'd like to make a purchase, please.

**Increase** (in KREES): *to get bigger.*

Your payments will increase from $5 a month to $10.

**Earnings** (ER ningz): *money you make.*

My earnings come from my job.

**Interest** (INT uh rest): *money paid for the use of money.*

A bank will charge interest for the money it lends.

# Same Words

Check the word in each row that is the same as the first word in the row. Go as fast as you can. Time yourself.

| | | | |
|---|---|---|---|
| **Increase** | Interest | Income | Increase |
| **Finance** | Finance | Finals | Balance |
| **Earnings** | Earrings | Earnings | Employ |
| **Interest** | Increase | Interest | Income |
| **Purchase** | Perhaps | Person | Purchase |

No. Correct _____

Time _____

## Scrambled Letters

The letters in each of the words are mixed up. Write the letters so they form words from the list at the top of page 25.

seanierc _____

stirente _____

ginrasen _____

ninface _____

capshure _____

## Missing Vowels

To finish the word, fill in the missing vowels. Write the complete word on the blank lines.

rnngs _____

fnnc _____

ntrst _____

prchs _____

ncrs _____

## Pick a Word

Underline the word that belongs in the space. Then write the word in the space.

A _____ is anything you buy.

    savings        purchase        firm

A rate _____ means the cost is going up.

    increase        limit        total

You must pay _____ on a loan.

    equal        terms        interest

He put his _____ into a savings account.

    debts        contracts        earnings

_____ means having to do with money or credit.

    Gross        Finance        Advance

**When your loan is confirmed, you'll get your money.**

## Words and Meanings

Say the credit word out loud and read its meaning. Read the sentence that follows. Then find and circle the credit word in the sentence.

**Confirmed** (kuhn FERMD): *checked out; OK'd.*

When your loan is confirmed, you'll get your money.

**Cancelled** (KAN suhld): *stopped; ended.*

You won't get money if your loan is cancelled.

**Bankrupt** (BANG kruhpt): *not having enough money to pay your bills with.*

That store lost so much money, it went bankrupt.

**Default** (di FAWLT): *not to pay as promised.*

If you don't pay each month, you are in default.

**Reference** (REF er uhnts): *someone who will say you pay your bills on time.*

May I use you as a reference?

## Same Words

Check the word in each row that is the same as the first word in the row. Go as fast as you can. Time yourself.

| | | | |
|---|---|---|---|
| **Bankrupt** | Interrupt | Banker | Bankrupt |
| **Default** | Default | Debited | Defeat |
| **Reference** | Receipt | Reference | Residence |
| **Confirmed** | Contract | Creditor | Confirmed |
| **Cancelled** | Current | Cancelled | Annual |

No. Correct _____

Time _____

## Letter Circles

The letters in each circle at right spell a word from the list at the top of page 27. Write the word below the circle.

## Missing Ink

Complete the words below by adding a curve or a straight line to each letter. Then write the words on the lines.

DEFAULT _____

BANKRUPT _____

CONFIRMED _____

REFERENCE _____

CANCELLED _____

## Pick a Word

Underline the word that belongs in the space. Then write the word in the space.

A loan that is _____ has been stopped.
    cancelled       current       firm

A loan that is _____ is OK.
    unpaid       confirmed       unsigned

You are _____ when you don't have enough money to pay your bills.
    bankrupt       balanced       financed

You need a good _____ to get a loan.
    debt       period       reference

If you don't pay a loan, you are in _____ .
    default       assets       contract

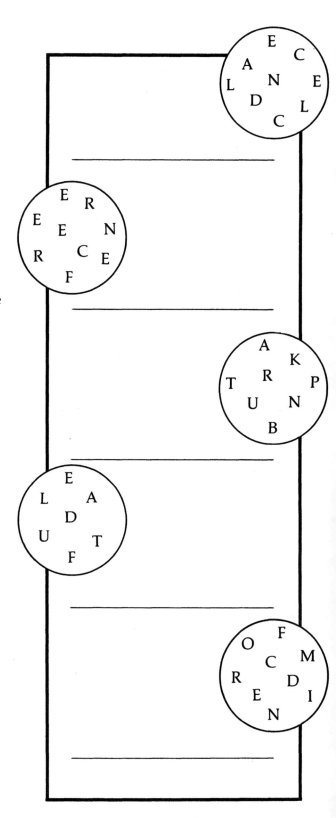

# Review

The 15 words from the list on page 22 fit into this puzzle. The first and last letters are given. The letters that go where the words cross are also given. Fill in the missing letters. Don't look back unless you have to.

# Test

Put a + by any sentence that is true. Put a ○ by any sentence that is not true.

_____ 1. A finance charge is a credit charge.

_____ 2. You are bankrupt if you can pay the balance.

_____ 3. A loan that is cancelled is OK.

_____ 4. You pay interest on a loan.

_____ 5. A loan that is confirmed has been stopped.

_____ 6. You need a good reference to get a loan.

_____ 7. You are in default when you pay in advance.

_____ 8. Your earnings are part of your income.

_____ 9. An account is a kind of plan.

_____ 10. *Amount* means "how much."

# Unit Four

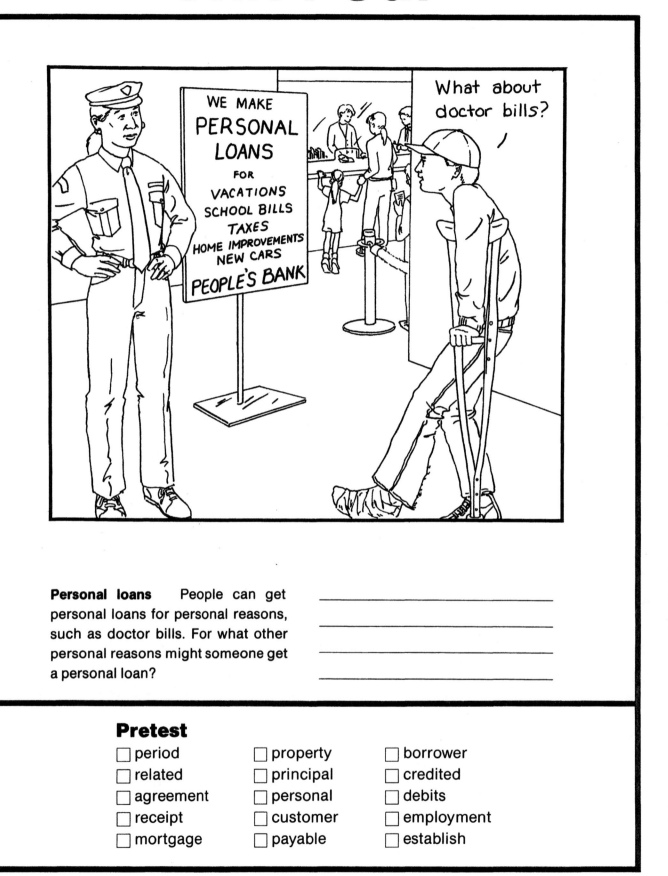

**Personal loans**   People can get personal loans for personal reasons, such as doctor bills. For what other personal reasons might someone get a personal loan?

_____

_____

_____

_____

## Pretest

- [ ] period
- [ ] related
- [ ] agreement
- [ ] receipt
- [ ] mortgage
- [ ] property
- [ ] principal
- [ ] personal
- [ ] customer
- [ ] payable
- [ ] borrower
- [ ] credited
- [ ] debits
- [ ] employment
- [ ] establish

**It will take 30 years to pay off your mortgage.**

# Words and Meanings

Say the credit word out loud and read its meaning. Read the sentence that follows. Then find and circle the credit word in the sentence.

**Period** (PIR ee uhd): *an amount of time.*
This loan must be paid within a period of one year.

**Related** (ri LAYT uhd): *in the same family.*
Are you two related?

**Agreement** (uh GREE muhnt): *a promise that you will do certain things; a contract.*
Our agreement is for you to pay $100 a month.

**Receipt** (ri SEET): *a paper that shows you paid for something.*
This receipt shows I paid for that bike.

**Mortgage** (MOR gij): *a loan to buy a house.*
It will take 30 years to pay off your mortgage.

# Same Words

Check the word in each row that is the same as the first word in the row. Go as fast as you can. Time yourself.

| | | | |
|---|---|---|---|
| **Receipt** | Receive | Repeat | Receipt |
| **Related** | Rebated | Related | Repossess |
| **Mortgage** | Morning | Monthly | Mortgage |
| **Period** | Period | Personal | Property |
| **Agreement** | Account | Agreement | Employment |

No. Correct _____

Time _____

## Word Wheel

Begin at Start. Find the word. Put a line between it and the next word. One word follows another. Write the words on the lines as you find them.

_____      _____

_____      _____

_____      _____

_____      _____

_____      _____

Start ▶ A G R E E M E N T P E R I O D R E C E I P T M O R T G A G E R E L A T E D

## Missing Vowels

To finish the word, fill in the missing vowels. Write the complete word on the blank lines.

rcpt _____

rltd _____

mrtgg _____

grmnt _____

prd _____

## Pick a Word

Underline the word that belongs in the space. Then write the word in the space.

A _____ is an amount of time.
    source        default        period

A _____ shows you paid for something.
    receipt        debt        lender

A contract is an _____ .
    advance        agreement        interest

Your mother is _____ to you.
    related        earnings        risk

A _____ is a loan to buy a house.
    statement        mortgage        business

**That customer comes here every week.**

# Words and Meanings

Say the credit word out loud and read its meaning. Read the sentence that follows. Then find and circle the credit word in the sentence.

**Property** (PROP ert ee): *things you own.*

My bike is my property.

**Principal** (PRIN suh puhl): *the amount of money you borrowed.*

My loan is for $500; so $500 is the principal.

**Personal** (PERS uhn uhl): *anything about you, such as your age or height.*

One personal question a bank asks is: "Are you married?"

**Customer** (KUHS tuh mer): *a person who buys something.*

That customer comes here every week.

**Payable** (PAY uh buhl): *can be paid.*

This bill is payable in ten monthly payments.

# Same Words

Check the word in each row that is the same as the first word in the row. Go as fast as you can. Time yourself.

| | | | |
|---|---|---|---|
| **Personal** | Purchase | Payable | Personal |
| **Property** | Penalty | Property | Principal |
| **Payable** | Payable | Playable | Personal |
| **Customer** | Consumer | Current | Customer |
| **Principal** | Personal | Principal | Principle |

No. Correct_____

Time _____

## Letter Circles

The letters in each circle at right spell a word from the list at the top of page 33. Write the word below the circle.

## Missing Ink

Complete the words below by adding a curve or a straight line to each letter. Then write the words on the lines.

PAYABLE _____

PROPERTY _____

CUSTOMER _____

PRINCIPAL _____

PERSONAL _____

## Pick a Word

Underline the word that belongs in the space. Then write the word in the space.

The _____ is the money you borrow.
    receipt        principal        income

Anyone who buys something is a _____.
    lender        reference        customer

This bill is _____ in ten monthly payments.
    payable        confirmed        unit

Anything you own is your _____.
    agreement        default        property

Questions about you are _____ questions.
    equal        personal        cancelled

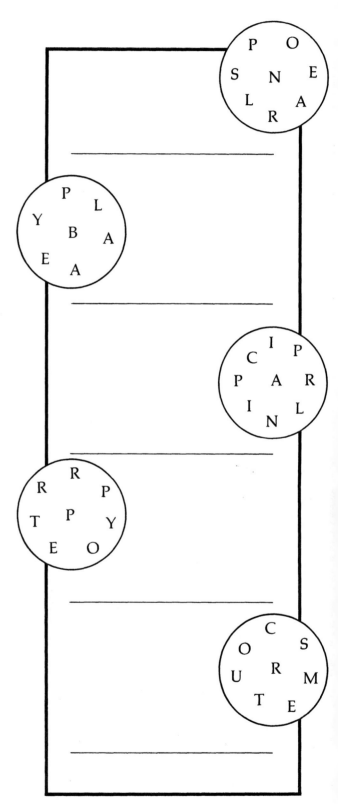

**What is your employment?**

# Words and Meanings

Say the credit word out loud and read its meaning. Read the sentence that follows. Then find and circle the credit word in the sentence.

**Borrower** (BAHR oh er): *a person who gets a loan.*

A borrower must promise to pay back a loan.

**Credited** (KRED uh tuhd): *marked to show you made a payment.*

The $5 you paid has been credited on your statement.

**Debits** (DEB uhts): *amounts you owe.*

The debits on this statement total $10.

**Employment** (im PLOI muhnt): *job; work done for pay.*

What is your employment?

**Establish** (is TAB lish): *to set up.*

You must first establish good credit to get a loan.

# Same Words

Check the word in each row that is the same as the first word in the row. Go as fast as you can. Time yourself.

| | | | |
|---|---|---|---|
| **Employment** | Enjoyment | Employment | Establish |
| **Credited** | Creditors | Current | Credited |
| **Establish** | Earnings | Establish | Employ |
| **Debits** | Debt | Dated | Debits |
| **Borrower** | Borrower | Buyer | Burrow |

No. Correct _____

Time _____

# Word Wheel

Begin at Start. Find the word. Put a line between it and the next word. One word follows another. Write the words on the lines as you find them.

_____

_____

_____

_____

_____

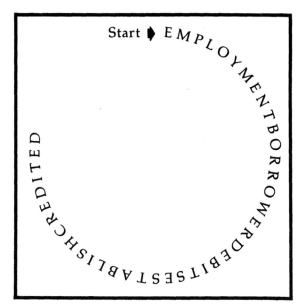

Start ▶ EMPLOYMENTBORROWERDEBITSESTABLISHCREDITED

# Scrambled Letters

The letters in each of the words are mixed up. Write the letters so they form words from the list at the top of page 35.

ditbes _____

atlehsisb _____

rowrobre _____

redicedt _____

tenlopmemy _____

# Pick a Word

Underline the word that belongs in the space. Then write the word in the space.

You need to _____ good credit to get a loan.

    establish        cancel        limit

Your _____ is the work you do.

    agreement      residence      employment

You are a _____ when you get a loan.

    lender      borrower      reference

Money you pay is _____ to your account.

    credited      charged      purchased

_____ are amounts you owe.

    Credits      Limits      Debits

## Unit Four
# Review

The 15 words from the list on page 30 fit into this puzzle. They go across and down. Use the clues and number of spaces to help you. Look back only if you have to. One is done for you.

**Across**

4. Marked to show you made a payment
6. To set up
8. The amount of money you borrow
10. Person who gets a loan
11. A paper that shows you paid for something
12. Anything you own
13. Can be paid

**Down**

1. A contract
2. A loan to buy a house
3. The work you do
4. Person who buys something
5. What your mother is to you
7. How much you owe
8. An amount of time
9. Anything about you

---

# Test

Answer these questions. Write *yes* or *no* in front of each question.

_____ 1. Is a mortgage the same as a receipt?

_____ 2. Does *payable* mean "no need to pay"?

_____ 3. Is the principal the amount of money borrowed?

_____ 4. Are debits amounts you owe?

_____ 5. Is personal property something that belongs to the city?

_____ 6. Are brothers and sisters related?

_____ 7. Is your boss your employment?

_____ 8. Can a customer also be a borrower?

_____ 9. Does *period* mean the same as *agreement*?

_____ 10. Is a statement credited when you owe money?

37

# Unit Five

**Credit Counselor (KOWN suh ler)**
Sometimes people don't use credit wisely. They owe more than they can pay. Credit counselors help people handle such problems. How might someone find a credit counselor?

_____

_____

## Pretest

- ☐ minimum
- ☐ maximum
- ☐ creditors
- ☐ penalty
- ☐ description
- ☐ installment
- ☐ annual
- ☐ residence
- ☐ deductions
- ☐ signature
- ☐ undersigned
- ☐ successive
- ☐ merchandise
- ☐ repossessed
- ☐ application
- ☐ occupation
- ☐ identification
- ☐ expiration
- ☐ authorization
- ☐ collateral

**Your creditors are waiting to be paid.**

# Words and Meanings

Say the credit word out loud and read its meaning. Read the sentence that follows. Then find and circle the credit word in the sentence.

**Minimum** (MIN uh muhm): *the least; the smallest.*

The minimum you can pay is $5 a week.

**Maximum** (MAK suh muhm): *the most; the largest.*

The maximum you can charge is $500.

**Creditors** (KRED uht erz): *those you owe money to.*

Your creditors are waiting to be paid.

**Penalty** (PEN uhl tee): *a fine.*

There is a $5 penalty if you pay your bill late.

**Description** (di SKRIP shuhn): *facts about something.*

Give a description of the car you want to buy.

# Same Words

Check the word in each row that is the same as the first word in the row. Go as fast as you can. Time yourself.

| Penalty | Period | Payable | Penalty |
|---|---|---|---|
| Description | Description | Deduction | Debited |
| Minimum | Maximum | Minimum | Mortgage |
| Creditors | Credited | Contract | Creditors |
| Maximum | Minimum | Maximum | Monthly |

No. Correct _____

Time _____

## Letter Circles

The letters in each circle at right spell a word from the list at top of page 39. Write the word below the circle.

## Missing Vowels

To finish the word, fill in the missing vowels. Write the complete word on the blank lines.

pnlty _____

mxmm _____

dscrptn _____

crdtrs _____

mnmm _____

## Pick a Word

Underline the word that belongs in the space. Then write the word in the space.

The _____ is the most you can charge.

    advance        principal        maximum

There is a _____ for paying your bill late.

    penalty        current        balance

You owe money to your _____ .

    debtors        creditors        savings

The _____ amount is the least you can pay.

    minimum        cancelled        personal

The bill had a _____ of his purchase.

    period        description        risk

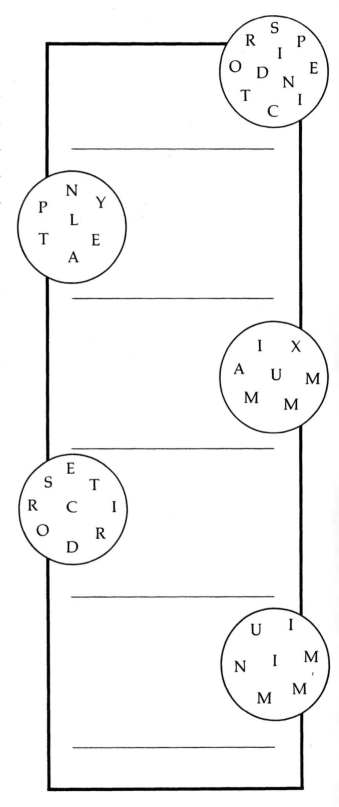

**My paycheck has too many deductions.**

## Words and Meanings

Say the credit word out loud and read its meaning. Read the sentence that follows. Then find and circle the credit word in the sentence.

**Installment** (in STAHL muhnt): *a payment.*

Did you pay this month's installment on your loan?

**Annual** (AN yoo uhl): *for one year.*

The annual rate is what you pay in one year.

**Residence** (REZ uh dens): *the place where you live: your address.*

On the application you must tell your residence.

**Deductions** (di DUHK shuhnz): *money taken out.*

My paycheck has too many deductions.

**Signature** (SIG nuh choor): *your name in your own writing.*

Put your signature here so we can cash your check.

## Same Words

Check the word in each row that is the same as the first word in the row. Go as fast as you can. Time yourself.

| **Deductions** | Reductions | Deductions | Default |
|---|---|---|---|
| **Installment** | Installment | Repayment | Income |
| **Annual** | Amount | Account | Annual |
| **Signature** | Successive | Statement | Signature |
| **Residence** | Reference | Residence | Repayment |

No. Correct _____

Time _____

## Scrambled Letters

The letters in each of the words are mixed up. Write the letters so they form words from the list at the top of page 41.

lunana _____

sidenecer _____

gnatisure _____

snoitcuded _____

tenmaillstn _____

## Missing Ink

Complete the words below by adding a curve or a straight line to each letter. Then write the words on the lines.

RESIDENCE _____

SIGNATURE _____

INSTALLMENT _____

ANNUAL _____

DEDUCTIONS _____

## Pick a Word

Underline the word that belongs in the space. Then write the word in the space.

An _____ is a payment on a loan.

    increase       installment       advance

Your _____ is where you live.

    business       receipt       residence

Your name in your writing is your _____.

    signature       statement       assets

There are many _____ from my paycheck.

    deductions       units       defaults

_____ means for one year.

    Monthly       Daily       Annual

**The store sign says, "Don't handle the merchandise!"**

## Words and Meanings

Say the credit word out loud and read its meaning. Read the sentence that follows. Then find and circle the credit word in the sentence.

**Undersigned** (UHN der sighnd): *the person whose name is written below.*

The undersigned agrees to pay for this loan.

**Successive** (suhk SES iv): *one right after another.*

I must make ten successive payments, one each month.

**Merchandise** (MER chuhn dighz): *things you buy.*

The store sign says, "Don't handle the merchandise!"

**Repossessed** (ree puh ZEST): *taken back.*

Your TV will be repossessed if you don't pay soon.

**Application** (ap luh KAY shuhn): *a form used to ask for a loan.*

Fill out an application if you want a loan.

## Same Words

Check the word in each row that is the same as the first word in the row. Go as fast as you can. Time yourself.

| | | | |
|---|---|---|---|
| **Merchandise** | Mortgage | Minimum | Merchandise |
| **Application** | Agreement | Application | Advance |
| **Undersigned** | Unsigned | Undersigned | Increased |
| **Successive** | Successive | Successful | Signature |
| **Repossessed** | Related | Reference | Repossessed |

No. Correct _____

Time _____

# Word Wheel

Begin at Start. Find the word. Put a line between it and the next word. One word follows another. Write the words on the lines as you find them.

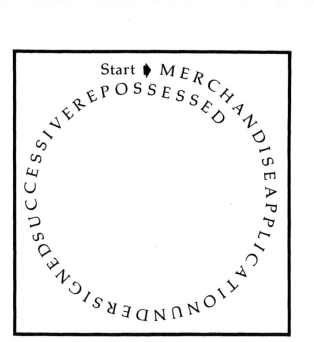

_____

_____

_____

_____

_____

# Missing Vowels

To finish the word, fill in the missing vowels. Write the complete word on the blank lines.

sccssv _____

ndrsgnd _____

pplctn _____

mrchnds _____

rpssssd _____

# Pick a Word

Underline the word that belongs in the space. Then write the word in the space.

_____ is anything you buy.

    Mortgage        Merchandise        Contract

The _____ is the one named below.

   undersigned      installments      descriptions

_____ means one after another.

    Balance        Successive       Creditors

You must fill out a loan _____ .

   employment      application      interest

_____ means taken back.

   Repossessed      Credited      Refunded

**May I see your identification, please?**

# Words and Meanings

Say the credit word out loud and read its meaning. Read the sentence that follows. Then find and circle the credit word in the sentence.

**Occupation** (ok yuh PAY shuhn): *your job, employment.*

Your occupation is what your job is.

**Identification** (igh dent uh fuh KAY shuhn): *something that shows who you are.*

May I see your identification, please?

**Expiration** (ek spuh RAY shuhn): *when something ends or runs out of time.*

The expiration date on your credit card shows when the card is no longer good.

**Authorization** (aw thuh ruh ZAY shuhn): *a written OK.*

The bank manager must give authorization before you get a loan.

**Collateral** (kuh LAT uh ruhl): *property you promise to give up if you do not pay.*

You can use your car for collateral to get a loan.

# Same Words

Check the word in each row that is the same as the first word in the row. Go as fast as you can. Time yourself.

| | | |
|---|---|---|
| **Authorization** | Authorization | Occupation |
| **Identification** | Inclination | Identification |
| **Collateral** | Creditors | Collateral |
| **Expiration** | Expiration | Exploration |
| **Occupation** | Occupying | Occupation |

No. Correct _____

Time _____

## Letter Circles

The letters in each circle at right spell a word from the list at the top of page 45. Write the word below the circle.

## Missing Ink

Complete the words below by adding a curve or a straight line to each letter. Then write the words on the lines.

EXPIRATION _____

OCCUPATION _____

COLLATERAL _____

IDENTIFICATION _____

AUTHORIZATION _____

## Pick a Word

Underline the word that belongs in the space. Then write the word in the space.

Your _____ shows who you are.

    merchandise       residence       identification

You'll need an _____ to get a loan.

    authorization       penalty       period

Use your car for _____ to get a loan.

    occupation       collateral       employment

Most credit cards have an _____ date.

    employment       earnings       expiration

Your job is your _____.

    agreement       occupation       application

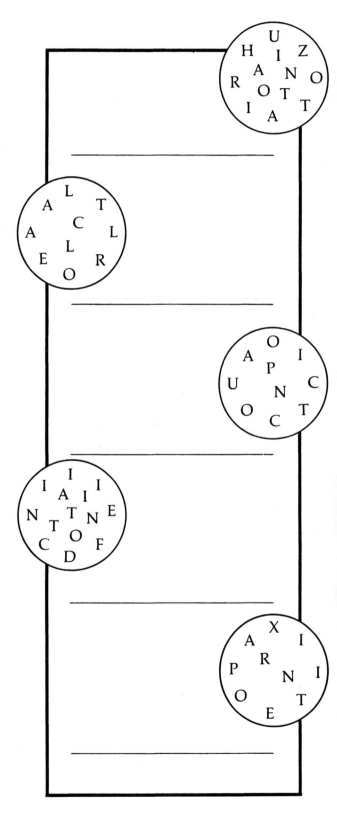

_____

_____

_____

_____

_____

# Review

The 20 words listed below are hidden in the puzzle. They are all printed in a straight line. But they may read across, up, down, backwards, or on a slant. Some words overlap. Circle the words as you find them. Then cross them off the list. One is done for you.

MINIMUM
MAXIMUM
CREDITORS
PENALTY
DESCRIPTION
INSTALLMENT
ANNUAL
RESIDENCE
DEDUCTIONS
SIGNATURE
UNDERSIGNED
SUCCESSIVE
MERCHANDISE
REPOSSESSED
APPLICATION
OCCUPATION
IDENTIFICATION
EXPIRATION
AUTHORIZATION
COLLATERAL

```
D W I H S O C O L L A T E R A L T H I
E M A T M N A S M L N E M E G P N I N
D Y I D E N T I F I C A T I O N B E S
U D T N H O E W O C B R U K C N O F T
C R E D I T O R S X M J O U C P M R A
T E L P A M T H Z A E V E R U D E E L
I O S H E W U G O D R H E X P E T P L
O W I I L N S M Y A C Y X A A A S O M
N L G H L E A P T T H S P R T P Q S E
S F N E A X D L E B A O I U I M R S N
E N A I I C D R T O N Q R P O U V E T
C G T M H C L M N Y D L A U N N A S T
N M U L B E U S T H I F T W O T H S E
E M R K N S U C C E S S I V E E N E P
D J E K I S T T X U E V O W D I S D R
I T E D E N G I S R E D N U X Y T Z E
S D I J F A Z Y D E S C R I P T I O N
E A P P L I C A T I O N X O F R E I E
R G H A U T H O R I Z A T I O N A M C
```

# Test

Answer these questions. Write *yes* or *no* in front of each question.

_____ 1. Is an annual payment made monthly?

_____ 2. Can merchandise ever be repossessed?

_____ 3. Do the undersigned write their signatures?

_____ 4. Do you pay a penalty for paying bills late?

_____ 5. Are lenders the same as creditors?

_____ 6. Is maximum the smallest amount?

_____ 7. Is a residence an authorization?

_____ 8. Do most credit cards have an expiration date?

_____ 9. Is collateral an installment?

_____ 10. Can you pay less than the minimum?

_____ 11. Do you need an application to get a loan?

_____ 12. Is your occupation the same as your work?

_____ 13. Do successive deductions come one after another?

_____ 14. Can you get credit with no identification?

# Guide to Phonetic Respellings*

Many of the words in this book are followed by respellings. The respellings show you how to say the words.

A respelling tells you three things about a word:
1. How many sounds, or syllables, the word has
2. Which syllable to stress
3. How to say each syllable

Look at the chart below. It shows you how to say each part of a respelling.

Now look at the word below. Then look at the respelling that follows it.

**example** (ig ZAM puhl)
1. How many syllables does *example* have? (3)
2. Which syllable should you stress? (ZAM)
3. How do you say each syllable? (ig) (ZAM) (puhl)

Say **example** (ig ZAM puhl) out loud. Then practice saying these respellings:

**practice** (PRAK tuhs)  **syllable** (SIL uh buhl)
**follow** (FAHL oh)  **phonetic** (fuh NET ik)

| If you see: | Say it like the: | In: | If you see: | Say it like the: | In: |
|---|---|---|---|---|---|
| (a) | a | pat | (m) | m | me |
| (ah) | a | father | (n) | n | no |
| (air) | air | fair | (ng) | ng | sing |
| (aw) | aw | paw | (oh) | oa | coat |
| (ay) | ay | day | (oi) | oy | boy |
| (b) | b | bee | (oo) | oo | too |
| (ch) | ch | chair | (or) | or | for |
| (d) | d | do | (ow) | ow | how |
| (e) | e | send | (p) | p | pay |
| (ee) | ee | see | (r) | r | row |
| (ehr) | err | merry | (s) | s | say |
| (er) | er | fern | (sh) | sh | she |
| (ear) | ear | hear | (t) | t | too |
| (f) | f | far | (th) | th | thin |
| (g) | g | go | (*th*) | th | the |
| (h) | h | he | (u) | u | put |
| (hw) | wh | where | (uh) | u | but |
| (i) | i | is | (v) | v | very |
| (igh) | igh | high | (w) | w | way |
| (j) | j | joy | (y) | y | you |
| (k) | k | key | (z) | z | zoo |
| (l) | l | lay | (zh) | s | treasure |

*All respellings are based on pronunciations found in *Webster's New Collegiate Dictionary*, 8th ed. (Springfield, Mass.: G. & C. Merriam Co., 1974). Pronunciations may differ in your community or your geographic region.